student WORKBOOK

AQA A2 Business Studies
Unit 4: The Business Environment and Managing Change

John Wolinski & Gwen Coates

Corporate aims and objectives
Understanding mission, aims and objectives 3

Assessing changes in the business environment
The relationship between businesses and the economic environment 8
The relationship between businesses and the political and legal environment 20
The relationship between businesses and the social environment 26
The relationship between businesses and the technological environment 31
The relationship between businesses and the competitive environment 34

Managing change
Internal causes of change 39
Planning for change 45
Key influences on the change process: leadership 50
Key influences on the change process: culture 54
Making strategic decisions 58
Implementing and managing change 62

Philip Allan Updates, an imprint of Hodder Education, an Hachette UK company, Market Place, Deddington, Oxfordshire, OX15 0SE

Orders
Bookpoint Ltd, 130 Milton Park, Abingdon, Oxfordshire, OX14 4SB
tel: 01235 827827   fax: 01235 400401
e-mail: education@bookpoint.co.uk

Lines are open 9.00 a.m.–5.00 p.m., Monday to Saturday, with a 24-hour message answering service. You can also order through the Philip Allan Updates website: www.philipallan.co.uk

ISBN 978-0-340-98599-1

© Philip Allan Updates 2009

All rights reserved; no part of this publication may be reproduced, stored in a retrieval system, or transmitted, in any form or by any means, electronic, mechanical, photocopying, recording or otherwise without either the prior written permission of Philip Allan Updates or a licence permitting restricted copying in the United Kingdom issued by the Copyright Licensing Agency Ltd, Saffron House, 6–10 Kirby Street, London EC1N 8TS.

Printed in Spain

Hachette UK's policy is to use papers that are natural, renewable and recyclable products and made from wood grown in sustainable forests. The logging and manufacturing processes are expected to conform to the environmental regulations of the country of origin.

Introduction

This student workbook is designed to:
- guide you through the content of the new AQA Business Studies A2 Unit 4: The Business Environment and Managing Change
- help to build your understanding of the three elements of this unit: corporate aims and objectives; assessing changes in the business environment; and managing change
- provide you with a good set of notes on all topic areas, to help your revision

For each section of the workbook there is:
- a set of notes providing an overview of the key aspects of the AQA specification
- a variety of questions covering the main topics

Remember that you will be using this workbook to assist your revision as the examination approaches, so when answering the questions:
- Use the notes provided in this workbook, but enhance them by using other sources, such as your textbook(s), notes from class sessions and references to business examples from your wider reading or knowledge of what is happening in the business world. Remember, the more detailed your answers, the more helpful they will be for your revision.
- Develop your arguments and use the skills that will be required in the examination, including application, analysis and evaluation – remember that every question in the Unit 4 examination is a 40-mark essay-style evaluative question.

Progress checklist

Corporate aims and objectives
Understanding mission, aims and objectives ☐

Assessing changes in the business environment
The relationship between businesses and the economic environment ☐
The relationship between businesses and the political and legal environment ☐
The relationship between businesses and the social environment ☐
The relationship between businesses and the technological environment ☐
The relationship between businesses and the competitive environment ☐

Managing change
Internal causes of change ☐
Planning for change ☐
Key influences on the change process: leadership ☐
Key influences on the change process: culture ☐
Making strategic decisions ☐
Implementing and managing change ☐

Corporate aims and objectives
Understanding mission, aims and objectives

A **mission statement** is a qualitative statement of an organisation's aims. It uses language intended to motivate employees and convince customers, suppliers and those outside the firm of its sincerity and commitment.

Corporate aims are the long-term intentions of a business. They determine the way in which an organisation will develop, providing a common purpose for everyone to identify with and work towards, and a collective view that helps to build team spirit and encourage commitment.

Corporate objectives are medium- to long-term targets that must be achieved in order to meet the stated aims of the business. They govern the targets for each division or department of the business; give a sense of direction to the whole organisation; act as a focus for decision making and effort, and as a yardstick against which success or failure can be measured; and encourage a sense of common purpose among the workforce.

Corporate strategies are the general approaches a company will use and the policies and plans it develops in order to achieve its corporate aims and objectives.

Key corporate aims and objectives

Corporate aims and objectives can be concerned with any of the following:
- survival
- profit
- growth
- diversification
- market standing
- meeting the needs of other stakeholders

Other examples of corporate aims and objectives include:
- maximising shareholder wealth
- maximising sales revenue
- social and environmental responsibility
- enhancing reputation through continuous technological innovation

Long-term and short-term corporate objectives

Long-term and **short-term corporate objectives** may differ for a number of reasons:
- A financial crisis is likely to encourage a firm to focus on short-term survival rather than, say, growth or market share.
- A long-term objective of improving profitability may be sacrificed in the short term in order to try to eliminate a competitor.
- In a recession, the immediate emphasis is likely to be on survival.

Corporate aims and objectives

- Changes in government policy may force a company to adopt different short-term priorities.
- Negative publicity from a faulty product or an environmental disaster will cause a firm to focus on improving its image in the short term.

Conflicting aims or interests of stakeholders

Stakeholders are individuals or groups with a direct interest in the activities and performance of an organisation.

The following list identifies the interests of the main stakeholder groups:
- Shareholders — high profit levels, a positive corporate image, long-term growth.
- Employees — job security, good working conditions, high levels of pay, promotional opportunities, job enrichment.
- Customers — high-quality products and services, low prices, good service, wide choice.
- Suppliers — regular/increasing orders, prompt payment, steady growth.
- Local community — employment opportunities, acting in a socially responsible manner.
- Government — efficient use of resources, employment and training, complying with legislation.

Businesses that focus solely on the needs of shareholders are taking a **shareholder approach** to business, in contrast to those that focus on trying to meet the needs of all stakeholders and have a **stakeholder approach**.

A **win–lose approach** is a business strategy that, in focusing on the needs of one stakeholder group, acts to the detriment of other stakeholder groups. The particular business context will influence how a business might prioritise the needs of the various stakeholder groups.

A **win–win approach** is a business strategy that aims to balance the needs of all stakeholder groups.

Questions

1 Explain what a mission statement is and why it might be advantageous for a business to have an effective mission statement.

Understanding mission, aims and objectives

2 Explain the terms 'corporate aim', 'corporate objective' and 'corporate strategy'.

3 Describe the relationship between corporate aims, corporate objectives and corporate strategies.

4 Consider why a firm's short-term objectives might differ from its longer-term objectives.

5 Distinguish between a company's shareholders and its stakeholders.

Corporate aims and objectives

6 Explain what it means if a company takes a stakeholder rather than a shareholder approach to its business.

7 What is the 'win–lose' approach in relation to stakeholders' needs?

8 How does the 'win–win' approach enable a business to meet the needs of all of its stakeholders?

9 Give examples of two business situations that illustrate conflicting stakeholder aims.

10 Identify three internal stakeholder groups and three external stakeholder groups.

Understanding mission, aims and objectives

Essay-style question

In order to answer the following question it is advisable first to undertake revision of the topic in the context of real-life businesses. Then, in the space provided, produce an outline plan of your answer. If you have time, use a separate sheet to write up the essay in full.

The founder of Greggs (the bakery chain) once suggested that its business strategy was one that put 'shareholders third in line behind employees and customers'. Is it sensible for Greggs, or any other business, to put its shareholders' interests behind those of other stakeholders such as customers and employees?

Assessing changes in the business environment
The relationship between businesses and the economic environment

PESTLE analysis

PESTLE is a framework for assessing the likely impact of the political, economic, social, technological, legal and environmental factors in the external environment of a business. The use of PESTLE analysis enables all the different influences in the general business environment to be classified into six categories.

PESTLE category	Examples of issues in each category that might affect business
Political factors	Government economic policies Government social policies Extent of government intervention
Economic factors	Business cycle Interest rates Exchange rates Level of inflation Level of unemployment Membership of the EU
Social factors	Ethical issues Impact of pressure groups Influence of different stakeholders Changing lifestyles
Technological factors	New products New processes Impact of change Costs of change
Legal factors	Legislation
Environmental factors	Environmental issues

The business cycle

The **business cycle** is the regular pattern of increasing and decreasing demand and output within an economy or of growth in gross domestic product (GDP) over time. It is characterised by four main phases: boom, recession, slump and recovery.

Possible causes of the business cycle are:
- changes in business confidence, leading to changes in the level of investment in fixed/non-current assets
- periods of inventory building and then de-stocking
- irregular patterns of expenditure on consumer durables, such as cars

The relationship between businesses and the economic environment

Characteristics of the business cycle
Each phase of the business cycle is characterised as follows:
- **Boom:** high levels of consumer demand, business confidence, profits, investment and business growth at the same time as rising costs, increasing prices and full capacity.
- **Recession:** falling levels of consumer demand, output, profit and business confidence; little investment, spare capacity, business closures and rising levels of unemployment.
- **Slump:** very low levels of consumer demand, investment and business confidence, an increasing number of businesses failing and high unemployment.
- **Recovery:** slowly rising levels of consumer demand, rising investment, increasing business confidence, higher profits, more business start-ups and falling levels of unemployment.

Business strategies in response to changes in the business cycle
The strategies a business might use will depend on which phase of the cycle the economy is in. For example, during a recession, many businesses will suffer declining demand. As a result they will wish to reduce production and improve efficiency. This may mean laying off workers, closing down factories or refocusing the business on its core activities — all of which will reduce costs and thus help the business to survive. However, although these strategies may be appropriate in the short term, they may be self-defeating in the longer term when demand begins to improve and a business finds it has insufficient trained staff or production capacity.

Economic growth
Economic growth means an increase in the level of economic activity or GDP. It provides favourable trading conditions and new business opportunities. It offers more security and certainty to firms and therefore provides them with more confidence in planning for the future. However, economic growth can result in serious negative externalities, such as pollution, congestion and harm to the environment.

Effects of economic growth on business
The effects of economic growth depend on whether the rate of growth is rapid, slowing down or actually decreasing, which reflects the various phases of the business cycle.
- **Impact on sales.** With higher levels of GDP, incomes in the economy are likely to be higher, which in turn is likely to lead to higher retail sales.
- **Impact on profits.** Higher incomes lead to greater demand for goods and services, which provides opportunities for firms to earn higher profits.
- **Impact on investment.** Higher demand for goods and services means that firms are more likely to invest in expanding their operations.
- **Impact on employment.** Once businesses are convinced that the increase in demand is sustainable, they are likely to want to recruit more workers.
- **Impact on business strategy.** The following business strategies are better suited to an environment of economic growth: expansion, new products and repositioning.

Assessing changes in the business environment

Interest rates

Interest rates are the cost of borrowing money and the return for lending money. They also measure the opportunity cost, to both individuals and firms, of spending money rather than saving it and receiving interest.

Implications of changes to the rate of interest
A fall in interest rates is likely lead to:
- an increase in demand for consumer goods
- an increase in demand for capital goods
- a fall in costs and a rise in profits
- a fall in the exchange rate of the pound, which is likely to lead to a fall in export prices and a rise in import prices

If interest rates rise, the opposite effects will occur.

Business strategies in response to changes in interest rates
Strategies will depend on whether the rate of interest is rising or falling, the nature of the goods or services provided and what else is happening within the economy. For example, if interest rates are rising, costs may rise. A business may be able to maintain its profit margin by increasing the price of its products. This is most likely to occur if demand for its products is price inelastic and/or if economic growth is positive.

Exchange rates

Exchange rates are the price of one country's currency in terms of another.

Implications for business of changes in exchange rates
The level of, and changes in, exchange rates affect businesses in different ways depending upon whether they are:
- businesses that export their goods to other countries
- businesses that sell their goods in the UK, competing against foreign imports
- businesses that purchase imported fuel, raw materials and components to use in the production of their own goods

Assuming that profit margins remain the same, an increase in the exchange rate may increase the price at which exports are sold abroad and reduce the price charged for imports in the UK. This in turn will affect revenue, competitiveness and profitability. The extent to which the changing prices of exports and imports will affect export sales and the purchase of imports depends on the price elasticity of demand.

However, the levels of export sales and import purchases are influenced not only by exchange rates, but also by a range of other factors, including reputation and quality, after-sales service, the reliability, design and desirability of the product, the overall packaging provided and payment terms.

The relationship between businesses and the economic environment

Business strategies in response to changes in exchange rates

The strategies a business might deploy will depend on whether exchange rates are rising or falling, what market the business operates in and whether it exports its goods to consumers in other countries, sells its goods in the UK in competition with foreign imports, or purchases imported fuel, raw materials and components to use in the production of its own goods. For example, if exchange rates are rising, a firm that sells its products in highly competitive markets abroad may decide not to increase its export prices and instead may reduce its profit margins.

Inflation

Inflation is an increase in the general level of prices within an economy.

Effects of inflation on business

- If interest rates are less than the rate of inflation, borrowing is encouraged. For highly geared firms and those with heavy borrowing, inflation reduces the real value of the sum they owe, making it easier to repay the loan.
- As inflation rises, so do property prices and the price of inventories. Thus balance sheets tend to look healthier.
- Firms find it easier to increase their prices when inflation is present because cost increases can be passed on to the consumer more easily.
- Higher prices may mean lower sales, depending upon the price elasticity of demand for particular products.
- The producers of major brands that tend to sell at premium prices may suffer as inflation makes consumers more aware of the price differentials.
- As consumers become more aware of prices, workers become far more concerned about the level of their real wages because, unless they obtain a pay rise at least as high as the rate of inflation, their real income will fall.
- Suppliers may increase their prices, adding further to a firm's costs and putting more pressure on the firm to increase its own prices.
- If inflation in the UK is relatively higher than inflation in other countries, the international competitiveness of UK firms may be reduced.
- As the future is uncertain, forecasts of sales revenue and profits will become very difficult and planning will be less reliable.
- When prices are changing quickly, businesses find it more difficult to keep track of competitors' pricing strategies.
- Cash flow is squeezed as the costs of new materials and equipment rise.

Business strategies in response to inflation

When deciding how to respond to inflation, a business must consider whether inflation is low or high and what the nature of the business and the products or services it offers is. Strategies will also depend on what is happening to the price of its supplies and the price of its competitors' products both at home and abroad.

For example, increasing fuel costs as a result of, say, rising oil prices can be more easily passed on to consumers in the form of higher prices during a period of inflation. Similarly, demands by trade unions for higher wages are more likely to be met if the subsequent increase in costs can be passed on in the form of higher prices.

Unemployment

Unemployment is a measure of the number of jobless people who want to work, are available to work, and are actively seeking employment.

Implications of high unemployment for business
- Consumer incomes fall, leading to lower sales.
- Workers have less bargaining power, meaning there is less pressure to increase wage levels.
- As demand falls, cost-saving strategies may be introduced.
- Lower demand is likely to lead to cutbacks or delays in investment projects.
- Lower demand and the need to reduce costs by reducing the workforce and investment may cause businesses to consider rationalisation as a strategy.

Business strategies in response to changes in the level of unemployment

Strategies will depend on the nature of the business, how efficient it is and whether its products are normal, luxury or inferior. For example, during a period of high unemployment, a firm selling an inferior product may find its sales rising considerably. To meet increased demand, it could try to increase its production capacity by, for example, increasing opportunities for existing employees to work overtime, or recruit more workers to staff an additional shift.

Globalisation and emerging markets

Globalisation has enabled financial and investment markets to operate internationally, largely as a result of deregulation and improved communications. Increasing globalisation is the result of:
- modern communication and the rapid spread of information technology (IT), which is changing the way companies, whether manufacturing or service providers, organise their activities
- increased trade, made easier by international agreements to lower tariff and non-tariff barriers on the export of manufactured goods, especially to rich countries

An **emerging market** is an international area that has the potential to grow and develop in terms of productive capacity, market opportunities and competitive advantage. Emerging markets include India, China and the countries of eastern Europe. They have the following implications for UK business:
- Their population size makes them potential major new markets.
- They offer market opportunities for both new products and well-established branded products.

The relationship between businesses and the economic environment

- There may be lower production costs because of cheaper labour and land rents and less stringent government controls.
- There will be new competition from firms in these countries.

Questions

1 Explain the implications of a recession for a firm selling inferior goods.

2 Explain the implications of a recession for a firm selling luxury products.

3 Consider why business confidence is such an important factor in influencing the business cycle.

4 Analyse the possible opportunities available to a retailer during an upturn or recovery in the business cycle.

Assessing changes in the business environment

5 Consider how a period of economic growth might affect the sales of consumer goods.

6 Consider how a period of economic growth might affect the sales of capital goods.

7 Explain three different ways in which a rise in interest rates might affect the demand for consumer goods.

8 Explain how a fall in interest rates might affect the demand for capital goods.

9 If a firm has loans, a rise in interest rates will lead to a rise in unit costs. In such a situation, how could the firm maintain its existing profit margin?

The relationship between businesses and the economic environment

10 What is the likely impact of a rise in the exchange rate of the pound on the price of UK exports abroad and the price of foreign imports into the UK?

11 If the exchange rate of the pound is rising, what is likely to be the impact on the costs and pricing of a UK firm that is dependent on imported raw materials?

12 Global Emporium Ltd is a medium-sized business involved in the export and import of products to and from destinations worldwide. Explain why fluctuating exchange rates might cause it difficulties.

13 At an exchange rate of £1 = $2.00, Global Emporium Ltd sells 2,000 products to the USA at a price equivalent to £12.00. If the exchange rate rises to £1 = $2.50, what effect might this have on its sales revenue? Explain your answer.

AQA A2 Business Studies: Unit 4   **15**

Assessing changes in the business environment

14 Global Emporium sells a range of products, including those that are price elastic and those that are price inelastic.

  a Analyse how a rise in the exchange rate of the pound is likely to affect its sales of price-elastic and price-inelastic products.

  b Suggest suitable strategies it might take in response to such a rise in the exchange rate of the pound.

15 Explain four adverse effects of inflation on a firm.

The relationship between businesses and the economic environment

16 Explain one possible benefit that inflation might have for both firms and individuals.

17 Explain three ways in which widespread unemployment in the economy is likely to have an adverse impact on businesses.

18 Explain two possible benefits to individual firms of the presence of widespread unemployment in the economy.

19 Although globalisation brings many advantages, it also threatens both manufacturing and service sector businesses in the UK. Explain why this is the case.

Assessing changes in the business environment

20 Explain two possible benefits and two possible problems of emerging markets, such as those in eastern Europe, for UK business.

....

....

....

....

....

....

Essay-style question

In order to answer the following questions it is advisable first to undertake revision of the topic in the context of real-life businesses. Then, in the space provided, produce outline plans of your answers. If you have time, use a separate sheet to write up the essay in full.

Select a business of your choice.

a Using the data provided, assess the extent to which success in the business is likely to have been influenced by changes in the economic variables in the 5 years between 2003 and 2008.

b Conduct research into the predicted rates of these economic variables for the next few years and evaluate how these predictions might influence the future performance of the business.

Data 1

UK economic growth (%), 2003–08

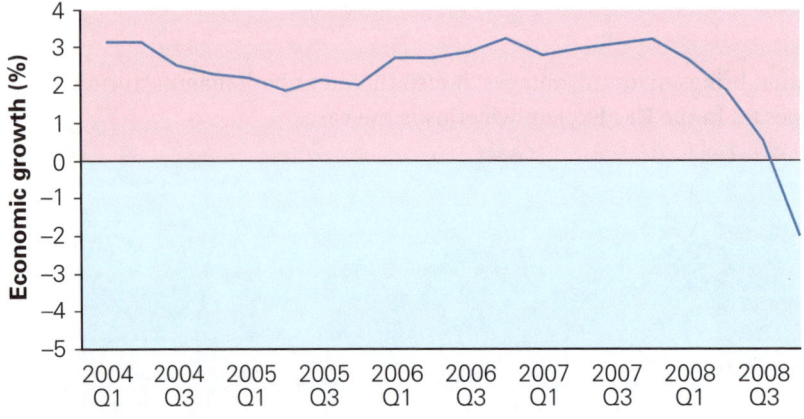

Source: **www.statistics.gov.uk**

The relationship between businesses and the economic environment

Data 2
Trends in UK interest rates (%)

Year	2003	2004	2005	2006	2007	2008
Interest rates	3.75	4.75	4.5	5.0	5.5	2.0

Source: **www.hm-treasury.gov.uk**

Data 3
Trends in the €/£ and $/£ exchange rates

Exchange rate	2003	2004	2005	2006	2007	2008
€s to the £	1.44	1.47	1.46	1.47	1.46	1.20
$s to the £	1.63	1.83	1.82	1.84	2.00	1.53

Source: **www.statistics.gov.uk**

Data 4
Trends in the annual UK rate of inflation (CPI)

	2003	2004	2005	2006	2007	2008
Inflation (%)	1.4	1.3	2.1	2.3	2.3	4.9

Source: **www.statistics.gov.uk**

Data 5
Annual UK rates of unemployment (%)

	2003	2004	2005	2006	2007	2008
Unemployment (%)	3.0	2.8	4.7	5.5	5.3	5.8

Source: **www.statistics.gov.uk**

The relationship between businesses and the political and legal environment

Government intervention means government policy based on the belief that government should exert a strong influence on the economy, rather than allowing market forces to dictate conditions. It includes the provision of products and services by government, economic policies such as monetary and fiscal policy, and regulation and legislation.

Most governments in the developed world provide a range of what are considered to be essential products and services, including education, health and housing.

Economic policies

Monetary policy means controlling the money supply and the rate of interest in order to influence the level of spending and demand in the economy.

Fiscal policy is the use of taxation and government expenditure to influence the economy.

Impact of monetary and fiscal policies on the economy and business

Monetary and fiscal policy can be used to influence the economy: for example, to reduce the effects of a recession and to encourage growth. The impact of a recession can be alleviated by:
- lowering interest rates to encourage investment and consumer spending
- cutting taxes to give people more spending power
- increasing government spending, which will have multiplier implications throughout the economy

The opposite measures might be used when the economy is booming, inflation is high and there are shortages of skilled labour.

While monetary and fiscal policies influence the overall level of demand in the economy, **supply-side policies** aim to increase the efficiency of supply and how markets work: for example, allowing the labour market to function efficiently by reducing the power of trade unions and improving incentives for people to find and retain jobs, increasing competition and reducing regulation.

Political decisions affecting trade and access to markets

The enlargement of the European Union (EU)

By 2007, the EU had expanded to 27 member states. Its main features include:
- free trade between member states and a common external tariff barrier for products from non-EU countries
- common technical standards for EU products
- harmonised VAT and excise duties
- the free movement of people and capital within the EU
- a European Central Bank and a single European currency (the euro) adopted by 17 of the 27 countries of the EU

Implications of the enlarged EU for UK business include:
- access to a market of 495 million people

The relationship between businesses and the political and legal environment

- opportunities for economies of scale, lower costs and increased specialisation
- more competition, which may lead to improved efficiency, lower costs and more innovation
- greater mobility of labour, giving firms a wider labour force to draw on
- firms are able to set up anywhere in the EU — for example, where costs are lower
- increased legislation and the need to meet common technical standards

Moves towards greater freedom of trade

The EU is an example of a **free trade area**: that is, a group of countries that agree to trade with each other without erecting any barriers to trade. This encourages competition between firms in the different member countries and, as a result, encourages greater efficiency and lower prices.

The World Trade Organization (WTO) is a group of over 153 countries that are committed to the encouragement of free and fair international trade through the elimination of trade barriers. It aims to ensure that 'trade flows as smoothly, predictably and freely as possibly'.

Legislation

Impact of legislation relating to businesses

Legislation and regulations protect those with weaker bargaining power and ensure a more ordered and predictable environment that is fairer for all parties concerned.

- **Employment legislation** falls into two broad categories: individual employment law, which aims to ensure that employees and employers act fairly in dealing with each other; and collective labour law, which aims to control industrial relations and trade union activity.
- **Consumer protection legislation** aims to safeguard consumers from exploitation or exposure to unsafe products or services.
- **Environmental protection legislation** includes EU directives on a range of issues including air quality and the collection, transport, recovery and disposal of waste. Legislation in this area is also aimed at preventing or minimising pollution from emissions.
- **Health and safety legislation** aims to provide a safe working environment for employees.
- **Competition policy** involves the use of legislation and regulation to ensure that all businesses are able to compete fairly with each other, and to limit the power of firms to take advantage of monopolies, mergers and restrictive practices.

Implications of legislation for business

- A firm's reputation may improve as a result of complying with legislation.
- Additional costs will be incurred in order to comply with the legislation.

Particular types of legislation will have a specific impact on certain aspects of business. For example, as a result of employment legislation:

- fewer working days may be lost due to strikes or industrial action
- equal opportunities legislation may mean the 'best' candidates are recruited
- employee motivation and the relationship between employees and employers may improve

Assessing changes in the business environment

Questions

1 Explain how fiscal policy and monetary policy are used to influence the level of demand in the economy.

2 Explain three ways in which a fall in interest rates might affect a business.

3 In 2008, the government reduced the rate of VAT and the rate of interest. Analyse the possible impact of these changes on UK retailers of price- and income-elastic goods and services during a recession.

The relationship between businesses and the political and legal environment

4 Analyse how a rise in the rates of income tax and of corporation tax might affect a business.

....

....

....

....

....

5 Using an example, explain the term 'supply-side policies'.

....

....

....

....

6 Explain three benefits for business of the UK's membership of the EU.

....

....

....

....

....

....

7 Analyse the significance of the UK's membership of the EU for a business based in the UK that buys its supplies from outside Europe and sells its products within the EU.

....

....

....

....

....

....

Assessing changes in the business environment

8 Explain the general purpose of legislation from a business point of view.

9 Explain one advantage to a business of each of the following areas of legislation:
   a employment

   b consumer protection

   c environmental protection

   d health and safety

10 Consider a common disadvantage for a business of each of the above areas of legislation.

Essay-style question

In order to answer the following question it is advisable first to undertake revision of the topic in the context of real-life businesses. Then, in the space provided, produce an outline plan of your answer. If you have time, use a separate sheet to write up the essay in full.

The UK recession in 2008 and 2009 led to a significant fall in demand for cars. UK car manufacturing directly employs approximately 190,000 people, but taking into account the components and retail sector, the industry as a whole employs approximately 850,000 people.

Discuss the range of economic policies available to the UK government and assess how successful these might be in improving the demand for cars and in averting the potential collapse of the car industry.

The relationship between businesses and the political and legal environment

The relationship between businesses and the social environment

Changes in the social environment

Demographic factors include the characteristics of human populations and population groups, including elements such as age, ethnicity, gender, religion and sexual orientation. Demographic changes influence two important aspects of business — employees and customers. Demographic change can be perceived as either an opportunity or a threat.

Environmental issues include the externalities that a firm creates — that is, the environmental effects of a firm's activities — which may be positive, such as job creation or providing a pleasing landscape around the factory, or negative, such as polluting the atmosphere with fumes or congesting the roads with lorries.

Opportunities provided when a firm assumes environmental responsibility

- **Marketing opportunities.** A good reputation in relation to environmental issues can act as a positive marketing tool that encourages consumers to choose one brand over another.
- **Financial opportunities.** Firms may find it easier to gain finance if they are able to point to a solid record of helping rather than damaging the environment.
- **Human resource opportunities.** A reputation for protecting the environment can have positive effects on potential employees' perceptions of a firm.

The changing nature of the ethical environment

Business ethics are the moral principles that should underpin decision making. Ethical behaviour involves actions and decisions that are seen to be morally correct. Examples of ethical dilemmas include:
- whether an advertising agency should accept a cigarette manufacturer as a client
- whether a firm should relocate to a country paying lower wages
- whether a firm should always pay suppliers on time or should delay as long as possible
- whether a firm should try to minimise its production costs and prices by using environmentally polluting processes

An **ethical code** is an instruction from an organisation to its employees to indicate how they should react to situations relating to moral values. **Ethical investment** refers to stock market investment only in firms that are seen as ethically sound.

Advantages of ethical behaviour

- Ethical behaviour can give companies a clear competitive advantage on which marketing activities can be based.
- Firms that adopt ethical practices may expect to recruit staff who are better qualified and motivated.
- Obtaining funds for investment purposes may be easier for a firm that behaves ethically.

The relationship between businesses and the social environment

Problems with ethical positions
- An ethical choice can incur extra costs and thus reduce profits.
- People have different views about what is ethical and these views change over time.
- In large organisations, it may be difficult to ensure that all staff follow the ethical code and to monitor adherence to it.
- As empowered workers take more decisions, it becomes harder to maintain a consistent company policy on ethical behaviour.

Corporate social responsibility (CSR) involves the duties of an organisation towards employees, customers, society and the environment. Examples of activities that would be viewed as socially responsible include:
- using sustainable sources of raw materials
- ensuring that suppliers operate responsibly (e.g. not using child labour)
- operating an extensive health and safety policy that is over and above the minimum legal requirements
- trading ethically and taking account of moral issues
- monitoring the effects of production on the environment by engaging in a continuous process of environmental management

Questions

1 'Business imposes external costs on society.' What does this mean?

2 Give two examples of how acting in an environmentally responsible way might:
  a benefit a firm

  b lead to problems for a firm

AQA A2 Business Studies: Unit 4   **27**

Assessing changes in the business environment

3 Explain three ways in which government could encourage business to reduce its polluting activities.

4 Analyse the effects on the airline industry of a proposal to charge passengers prices that reflect environmental as well as general business costs.

5 Explain the term 'ethical behaviour' and provide two examples of ethical dilemmas that might occur in business.

The relationship between businesses and the social environment

6 What is the purpose of an ethical code?

7 Explain two factors that might affect the ability of a firm to adopt an ethical stance.

8 Outline two advantages and two possible disadvantages to a business of operating in an ethical manner.

9 Explain the term 'corporate social responsibility' and provide two examples of a firm acting in a socially responsible manner in relation to its employees and two examples in relation to its customers.

Assessing changes in the business environment

10 Outline two advantages and two disadvantages to a firm of accepting its social responsibility.

Essay-style question

In order to answer the following question it is advisable first to undertake revision of the topic in the context of real-life businesses. Then, in the space provided, produce an outline plan of your answer. If you have time, use a separate sheet to write up the essay in full.

Many companies, including Starbucks, B&Q and the Body Shop, place great emphasis on their approach to social responsibility. To what extent might it be argued that their approaches are simply another strategy for increasing consumer demand and customer loyalty?

The relationship between businesses and the technological environment

Technological change means adapting new applications of practical or mechanical sciences to industry and commerce.

Information technology is the creation, storage and communication of information using microelectronics, computers and telecommunications.

Benefits of technological change

The benefits of technological change include:
- improved efficiency and reduced waste
- better products and services
- new products and materials
- advances in communication
- improved working environment
- higher living standards

Issues to consider when introducing new technology

A business should consider the following issues when introducing new technology:
- the cost of keeping up to date with the latest technology
- knowing what new technology to buy and when to buy it
- ensuring that new technology is compatible with existing technology
- in most cases, the introduction of new technology will replace, or change the nature of, jobs, so the cooperation of the workforce is essential
- the new skills required and the implications for recruitment and training and their associated costs
- short-term difficulties, such as a decline in productivity, while employees become skilled at using the new technology and teething problems are ironed out
- marketing opportunities
- the culture of the business
- the processes and systems used within the business

Questions

1 Identify two examples of technological change in:

   a the primary sector of industry

   b the secondary sector of industry

   c the tertiary sector of industry

AQA A2 Business Studies: Unit 4

Assessing changes in the business environment

2 Explain what is meant by technological change in relation to:

a innovation in processes

b innovation in products

3 Outline two benefits of the use of new technology to:

a consumers

b firms

4 Outline two problems for business that may result from the introduction of new technology.

5 Using a business example of your choice, analyse the main factors that might encourage the business to introduce new technology.

The relationship between businesses and the technological environment

Essay-style question

In order to answer the following question it is advisable first to undertake revision of the topic in the context of real-life businesses. Then, in the space provided, produce an outline plan of your answer. If you have time, use a separate sheet to write up the essay in full.

Using business examples you are familiar with, assess the extent to which technological change might have an impact on the following aspects of a business: marketing opportunities, business culture and the processes and systems used within a business.

The relationship between businesses and the competitive environment

The competitive structure

Some businesses operate in very competitive markets, where there are many small firms, each selling only a very small proportion of the total market sales. Other businesses operate in markets that tend to be dominated by a few large firms, each selling a significant proportion of the total market sales. The four main competitive structures that businesses operate in are monopoly, oligopoly, monopolistic competition and perfect competition.

Reasons for changes in competitive structure

Changes to competitive structure come about as a result of:
- **The emergence of new competitors.** This can occur because a new business enters the industry. In order to compete, existing businesses will need to ensure that their products or services are of an appropriate quality, are priced and promoted appropriately and have their own unique selling points. In some industries, barriers to entry prevent or deter new firms from entering and setting up in business.
- **The development of dominant businesses.** From being a relatively small player in a market, a business can develop into a dominant business as a result of takeover or merger activity.
- **Changes in the buying power of customers.** The power of customers is related to their ability to influence the price that they pay. The extent to which an individual customer has power over a business will depend on whether he/she is one among many customers, each purchasing a small proportion of total sales, or one of only a small number of customers, each of whom purchases a large proportion of total sales.
- **Changes in the selling power of suppliers.** The power of suppliers is related to their ability to influence the prices they will receive for their supplies. The more concentrated and controlled the source of supply, the more power it is likely to wield in the market. This will be determined by whether the supplies that a business requires are purchased from a firm for which there are many alternative competing suppliers or from a single firm that is the only source of the supply.

Responses to changes in the competitive environment
- If a new competitor emerges in the market, a business might try to diversify into other markets or consider merging with or taking over another business in order to establish itself as a dominant business in the market.
- If a business currently sells to a single buyer, its strategy might be to find more buyers in order to reduce the power of any one buyer.
- If a supplier has too much power over a business, one possibility is for the business to find alternative sources of supply.

Concentration ratios are one way of measuring the degree of concentration in an industry: that is, whether a few large, or a large number of small, firms are responsible for the majority of sales in the market.

The relationship between businesses and the competitive environment

Questions

1 In relation to the competitive environment in which business operates, briefly explain the characteristics of:

a a monopoly situation

b an oligopoly situation

c a monopolistic competition situation

d a perfect competition situation

2 Identify the various barriers to entry that might operate in monopoly or oligopoly markets.

Assessing changes in the business environment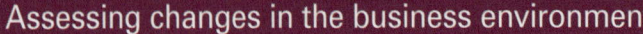

3 One way to analyse the competitive environment of a firm is to use Porter's five competitive forces model. Identify and explain each of these five forces.

....

....

....

....

....

....

....

....

....

4 Analyse four possible ways in which the competitive structure of an industry might change.

....

....

....

....

....

....

....

....

....

....

....

....

The relationship between businesses and the competitive environment

5 a The 5-firm concentration ratios for the tobacco products and furniture industries are 99% and 4% respectively. What does this mean?

....
....
....
....

b The 5-firm concentration ratios for the motor vehicle industry and clothing industry are 63% and 4% respectively. Analyse why the motor vehicle industry is so highly concentrated compared to the clothing industry.

....
....
....
....
....
....
....
....
....
....
....
....
....
....

Assessing changes in the business environment

Essay-style question

In order to answer the following question it is advisable first to undertake revision of the topic in the context of real-life businesses. Then, in the space provided, produce an outline plan of your answer. If you have time, use a separate sheet to write up the essay in full.

The banking industry is an oligopoly market. A merger between Lloyds TSB and HBOS was finalised in January 2009. The newly named Lloyds Banking Group will control about 25% of British customers' personal bank accounts and about 28% of the mortgage market. In order to permit the merger of HBOS and Lloyds TSB, competition law was set aside by the UK government because it was felt that the deal would help maintain the stability of the banking sector. The Treasury will own just under 45% of the merged bank. At the end of 2008, the Office of Fair Trading commented that there could be a 'substantial lessening of competition' in personal current accounts, bank services for smaller firms, and the mortgage market as a result of the merger.

Assess the potential effects of this development on other firms in the banking industry and the possible impact on customers.

Managing change
Internal causes of change

Organisational change can come about through a change in the size of the business, the introduction of new owners and leaders, and poor business performance.

Change in organisational size

Internal and external growth
Internal or **organic growth** occurs when a firm expands its existing capacity or range of activities by extending its premises or building new factories from its own resources, rather than by integration with another firm.

External growth comes about when two or more businesses integrate via a merger or takeover. A **merger** is where two or more firms agree to come together under one board of directors. A **takeover** (or acquisition) is where one firm buys a majority shareholding in another firm and therefore assumes full management control.

External growth is usually the fastest way to achieve growth, but, given the problems of integrating two separate organisations, it can be risky.

Types of integration
External growth, whether by merger or takeover, can be classified into three broad types of integration.

Vertical integration is the coming together of firms in the same industry but at different stages of the production process. It includes backward and forward integration. Vertical integration:
- removes the uncertainty of dealing with external suppliers and retailers
- facilitates cost savings in both technical and marketing areas
- builds barriers to entry for new competitors
- enables the profit margins of suppliers and/or retailers to be absorbed

Horizontal integration is the coming together of firms operating at the same stage of production and in the same market. Firms involved in horizontal integration are usually potential competitors. Horizontal integration results in:
- economies of scale
- lower unit costs
- reduced competition
- increased market share

Conglomerate integration is the coming together of firms operating in unrelated markets. It results in the spreading of risks through diversification. It may lead to the sharing of good practice between different areas of the business, although, in some cases, management has little or no expertise in the newly acquired business area.

Retrenchment
Retrenchment means the cutting back of an organisation's scale of operations. It can occur by:
- halting recruitment or offering early retirement or voluntary redundancy
- delayering
- closing a factory, outlet or division of the business
- making targeted cutbacks and redundancies throughout the business

New owners and leaders

Managing growth
The growth of a business often means that owners, who have previously been in complete control of all aspects of a business, have to plan for, and then adjust to, handing over responsibility to others. This is because in a large organisation:
- leadership requires a much less hands-on approach
- there is a need to delegate much more
- the task of controlling and coordinating activities is much more complex
- without strong and effective management, growth can result in a loss of direction and control
- managing and motivating a large team requires very different skills from those needed in a medium-sized business
- introducing a solid organisational structure, having an effective management team and carrying out detailed financial and operational planning and forecasting are vital

Bringing in a management team
Most businesses, as they grow, need restructuring. A bigger company needs managers to take control of departments and a hierarchy that includes people with the expertise and the time to drive it forward. In many cases, the expertise to build and manage a new structure comes from outside the business. Private investors and venture capital firms usually evaluate management structures and the existing expertise of management before deciding whether to invest. They often insist on recruiting new or interim management. This can be seen as a way of taking control away from the founder, but it is also a way of protecting their investment in the business by ensuring that skills gaps are plugged and necessary structures and experience are in place.

Poor business performance
Internal change can also come about as a result of the poor performance of a business. Poor performance may lead to a reduction in the size of the business and a change in ownership or in leaders and senior managers.

Internal causes of change

Questions

1 A business can grow organically or by external means. Distinguish between these different approaches to growth.

2 What is the difference between a merger and a takeover?

3 Explain the following types of external growth and, in each case, give one possible motive for such an approach to growth:
   a vertical integration

   b horizontal integration

   c conglomerate integration

4 Give two examples of each of the following:
   a horizontal integration

b conglomerate integration

c forward vertical integration

d backward vertical integration

5 Consider why businesses like the Arcadia Group (which owns Topshop and Littlewoods) and Gap might have chosen to expand through horizontal integration, while other businesses might choose to expand by diversification.

6 Define the term 'retrenchment' and identify two types of retrenchment.

7 Analyse one positive and one negative effect of retrenchment on employees in an organisation.

Internal causes of change

8 How might the role of the leader/manager of a large business differ from that of the owner of a small business?

9 The rapid growth of a business can lead to a loss of direction and control. Analyse why this might occur and how it might be avoided.

10 Analyse why poor performance is likely to result in internal changes to an organisation.

Managing change

Essay-style question

In order to answer the following question it is advisable first to undertake revision of the topic in the context of real-life businesses. Then, in the space provided, produce an outline plan of your answer. If you have time, use a separate sheet to write up the essay in full.

In 2002 the US computer giant Hewlett-Packard completed a merger with Compaq. At the time, there was talk of huge benefits, including greater synergies, economies of scale, improved market share and improved profit margins. The merger resulted in a loss of 15,000 jobs (about 10% of the new company's workforce). The combined group's shares remained stubbornly low and the expected benefits were not realised.

Using this example and any others with which you are familiar, assess the potential implications for business of external growth as compared with organic growth.

Planning for change

The purpose and value of corporate plans

Corporate plans are strategies detailing how a firm's aims and objectives will be achieved. They comprise medium- and long-term actions. Corporate plans:
- clarify the role of each department in contributing to meeting overall aims and objectives
- allow for better coordination of activities
- help to identify the resources required and so make it easier to raise finance by providing a clear plan of action, indicating how and why investment is required

The success of a corporate plan depends on:
- whether it is the right plan for the business in its present circumstances
- whether there are adequate resources to implement the plan
- the probable actions and reactions of competitors
- how changes in the external environment are likely to affect the plan

Assessing internal and external influences on corporate plans: SWOT analysis

SWOT analysis is a technique that allows a business to assess its overall position. It consists of:
- **An internal audit.** This is an assessment of the strengths and weaknesses of the business in relation to its competitors. It represents the present position of the business.
- **An external audit.** This is an assessment of the opportunities and threats the business faces in the general business environment. It represents the future potential of the business. A PESTLE analysis is often used in an external audit.

Advantages of SWOT analysis
- It highlights current and potential changes in the market and encourages an outward-looking approach.
- It encourages firms to develop and build upon existing strengths.
- It relates the present position to the future potential of a business and is thus an excellent basis on which to make decisions.
- By determining the organisation's position, it influences the strategy that will be employed in order to achieve the organisation's aims and objectives.

Disadvantages of SWOT analysis
- It can be time consuming.
- Internal and, particularly, external factors can change rapidly.

Contingency planning

Contingency planning means preparing for unexpected and, usually, unwelcome events that are, however, reasonably predictable and quantifiable. It is a costly activity. In large firms, it can involve huge numbers of highly qualified staff in assessing risk and planning what to do if

Managing change

things go wrong. Like any other form of insurance, it reduces risk but may seem like a waste of money if nothing ultimately goes wrong.

Crisis management means responding to a sudden event that poses a significant threat to a firm.

Questions

1 Explain what a corporate plan is and what the various stages in the corporate planning process are.

2 How might a business benefit from having a corporate plan?

3 Why might a corporate plan fail?

4 How do strategic decisions differ from tactical decisions?

Planning for change

5 Explain the term 'SWOT analysis' and the various elements of it.

6 Why might a SWOT analysis benefit a business?

7 Give two business examples of each of the four elements of a SWOT analysis.

8 Consider how a SWOT analysis is affected by uncertainty and the time period under consideration.

Managing change

9 Explain:

a the term 'contingency planning'

....

....

b the various steps involved in the contingency planning process

....

....

....

....

10 Because, in general, things rarely go wrong, consider how the costs of contingency planning can be justified.

....

....

....

....

....

Essay-style question

In order to answer the following question it is advisable first to undertake revision of the topic in the context of real-life businesses. Then, in the space provided, produce an outline plan of your answer. If you have time, use a separate sheet to write up the essay in full.

Using a business example of your choice, assess how useful it is to analyse the internal and external influences facing the business, even when these influences are subject to constant change and uncertainty.

....

....

....

Planning for change

Key influences on the change process: leadership

Leadership means deciding on the direction for a company in relation to its objectives and inspiring staff to achieve those objectives. **Management** means getting things done by organising other people to do them.

Leadership styles

- **Authoritarian leadership:** a leadership style in which communication tends to be one-way and top-down.
- **Paternalistic leadership:** a leadership style in which employees are consulted but decision making remains firmly at the top.
- **Democratic leadership:** a leadership style involving two-way communication and considerable delegation.
- **Laissez-faire leadership:** a leadership style that abdicates responsibility and takes a 'hands-off' approach.
- BUREAUCRATIC

McGregor's Theory X and Theory Y

A Theory X manager assumes that workers:
- are lazy, dislike work and are motivated by money
- need to be supervised and controlled or they will underperform
- have no wish or ability to help make decisions or take on responsibility
- are not interested in the needs of the organisation and lack ambition

A Theory Y manager assumes that:
- workers have many different needs, enjoy work and seek satisfaction from it
- workers will organise themselves and take responsibility to do so
- poor performance is likely to be due to monotonous work or poor management
- workers wish to, and should, contribute to decisions

Internal and external factors influencing leadership style

Influences on leadership style are illustrated in the diagram opposite. Most influences are internal factors, although 'The particular situation' could include external factors, such as the influence of the competitive market in which the business operates and whether a rival firm is attempting a takeover.

The culture of an organisation affects, and is affected by, the style of leadership, which in turn is a major influence on the degree and effectiveness of delegation and consultation. The culture of an organisation also affects the degree of resistance to change and therefore the ability of new leaders to introduce new strategies.

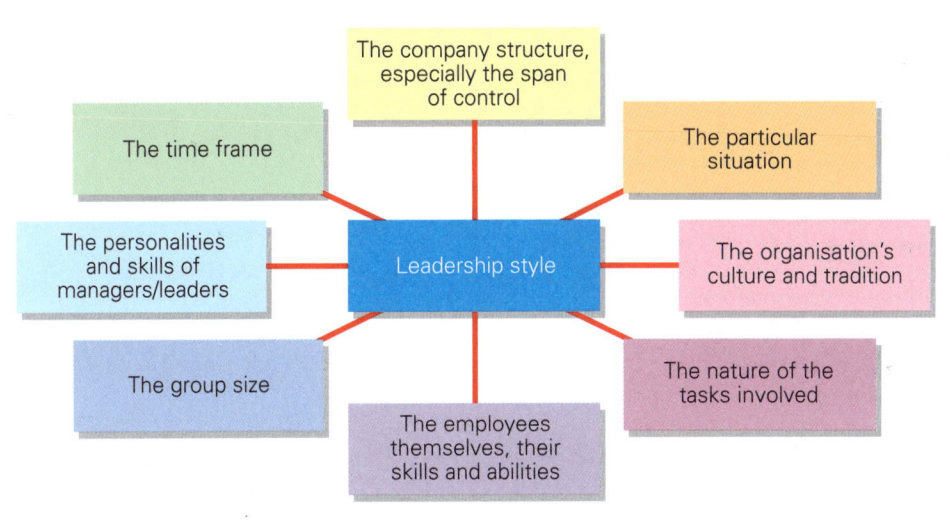

Key influences on the change process: leadership

Influences on the choice of leadership style

- The company structure, especially the span of control
- The time frame
- The particular situation
- The personalities and skills of managers/leaders
- Leadership style
- The organisation's culture and tradition
- The group size
- The nature of the tasks involved
- The employees themselves, their skills and abilities

The role of leadership in managing change

Successful management of change requires effective leadership in order to ensure that changes to business strategy and operations are effectively anticipated, organised, introduced and evaluated.

Questions

1 What is the difference between leadership and management?

....
....
....

2 Describe the main characteristics of each of the following leadership styles:
   a authoritarian

....
....
....

   b paternalistic

....
....
....

Managing change

c democratic

d laissez-faire

3 Explain the difference between McGregor's Theory X and Theory Y managers.

4 Consider the links between Theory X and Theory Y management styles and the various leadership styles.

Key influences on the change process: leadership

5 The effectiveness of delegation and consultation is an important influence on motivation. Analyse how this is linked to the various leadership styles.

Essay-style question

In order to answer the following question it is advisable first to undertake revision of the topic in the context of real-life businesses. Then, in the space provided, produce an outline plan of your answer. If you have time, use a separate sheet to write up the essay in full.

Jack Welch was Chairman and Chief Executive Officer of General Electric (GE) between 1981 and 2001. He gained a reputation for unique leadership strategies. His view was that 'Managers slow things down. Leaders spark the business to run smoothly, quickly. Managers talk to one another, write memos to one another. Leaders talk to their employees, talk with their employees, filling them with vision, getting them to perform at levels the employees themselves didn't think possible. Then they simply get out of the way.'

Using your knowledge of businesses such as GE, to what extent do you agree with the view that it is impossible to distinguish between a senior executive's role as a manager and his/her role as a leader?

Key influences on the change process: culture

Types of organisational culture

Organisational culture is the unwritten code that affects the attitudes and behaviour of staff, approaches to decision making and the leadership style of management. Different organisations have different types of culture, including:

- **Power culture.** A powerful individual or small group determines the dominant culture. Power culture is like a web with a ruling spider. Those in the web are dependent on a central power source. Rays of power and influence spread out from the central figure or group.
- **Role culture.** An organisation with a role culture is often referred to as a bureaucracy. Such organisations are controlled by procedures and role descriptions. Coordination is from the top and job positions are important. Such organisations value predictability and consistency, and may find it hard to adjust to change.
- **Task culture.** This is where the organisation's values are related to a job or project. Task culture is usually evident in small teams or organisations cooperating to deliver a project. The emphasis is on results and getting things done. Individuals are empowered with independence and control over their work.
- **Person culture.** This culture occurs in universities and in professions, such as accountancy and legal firms, where the organisation exists as a vehicle for people to develop their own careers and expertise. The individual is the central point. If there is a structure, it exists only to serve the individuals within it.
- **Bureaucratic culture.** Organisations with bureaucratic cultures tend to have generalised and non-commercial goals. They have hierarchical structures and there is an emphasis on precisely defined roles, responsibilities and procedures (rather like a role culture). People tend to be risk averse and anxious to avoid mistakes.
- **Entrepreneurial culture.** Organisations with entrepreneurial cultures tend to emphasise results and rewards for individual initiative (rather like a power culture); risk taking; quantitative and financial goals; a task culture with flexible roles; and a relatively flat and flexible structure, which gives a degree of local control.

Changing organisational ~~structure~~

Reasons for changing organisational culture

A business may seek to change its culture because of:
- a change in the external environment
- a merger or takeover
- a change in leadership

Problems of changing organisational culture

Problems that a company might face when seeking to change its culture include:
- the existing organisational culture, which when challenged may produce strong resistance to change

Key influences on the change process: culture

- leaders and senior managers, who may not communicate the case for cultural change effectively
- inadequate training, which may not prepare employees effectively for cultural change
- inappropriate recruitment, which may lead to the wrong people being employed
- inappropriate organisational structure, which may constrain entrepreneurial flair and risk taking

The importance of organisational culture

Organisational culture is important for several reasons:
- It determines how firms respond to changes in their external environment.
- It has an important bearing on an organisation's behaviour and performance.
- It influences organisational structure (as well as being influenced by it).
- It is influential in the development of mission statements.
- It affects leadership styles and has a major effect on the degree of, and effectiveness of, delegation and consultation.
- It affects how well a business is able to introduce change.
- It influences the success of a business.

Questions

1 Define the term 'organisational culture' and explain each of the following types of organisational culture: power culture, role culture, task culture and person culture.

Managing change

2 Distinguish between a bureaucratic culture and an entrepreneurial culture.

3 How might an organisation's culture influence:
  a its attitude to risk taking?

  b the degree of resistance to change in that organisation?

4 Identify:
  a a possible reason for organisational change

  b how such change might be brought about

  c a problem of changing the culture of an organisation

Key influences on the change process: culture

5 Analyse why an organisation's culture is important.

Essay-style question

In order to answer the following question it is advisable first to undertake revision of the topic in the context of real-life businesses. Then, in the space provided, produce an outline plan of your answer. If you have time, use a separate sheet to write up the essay in full.

DaimlerChrysler was founded in 1998 when the German Mercedes manufacturer, Daimler-Benz, merged with the US-based Chrysler Corporation. The two businesses appeared to complement each other because they operated in different segments of the car market and were prominent in different geographical markets. However, Mercedes struggled to blend the contrasting business cultures of the two businesses and the deal failed to produce the transatlantic automotive powerhouse that was anticipated. In 2007, DaimlerChrysler sold Chrysler to a private equity organisation.

Evaluate the extent to which conflicting organisational cultures might play a part in the failure of a merger, such as that described above.

Making strategic decisions

Information management is the application of management techniques to collect information, communicate it within and outside the organisation, and process it to enable managers to make quicker and better decisions.

Different approaches to decision making and their value

The scientific approach
Scientific decision making means taking a logical and research-based approach to decision making. Benefits of such an approach include the following:
- It provides a clear sense of direction.
- Decisions are based on comparisons between alternative approaches.
- It is likely that more than one person will be involved in the process.
- Decisions are monitored continually and reviewed.
- The approach is flexible and the process can be reviewed and changed.
- If all decisions are based on rational thinking, overall success is more probable.
- It is easier to defend a policy developed on the basis of good planning.

Hunch, or the intuitive approach
Hunch, or the intuitive approach to decision making, means decisions being made on the basis of a gut feeling or the personal views of the manager. Few decisions can be made on a purely objective basis; most include a subjective element based on managerial experience and intuition. Thus the benefits of using hunches are, in general, the problems of a scientific approach, which include the following:
- A scientific approach is a very expensive process.
- A scientific approach is time consuming.
- Data collected in a scientific approach to decision making might be flawed.
- Invariably, scientific decisions are based on past information.

Deciding which approach to use
The following factors are critical in deciding which approach to use:
- the speed at which a decision needs to be made
- the information available
- the size of the business
- the predictability of the situation
- the character of the leader or the culture of the company

Influences on corporate decision making
- **Ethical positions.** A business may adopt a seemingly ethical position, which is popular with consumers and is likely to lead to increased sales. Whether this is a reflection of the business adopting a 'real' ethical position or a 'perceived' one — as a PR exercise in order to gain consumer loyalty and increase sales — is debatable.
- **Resources.** The resources available to a business, whether financial, human or physical, have a huge influence on corporate plans and corporate decisions.

Making strategic decisions

- **The relative power of the stakeholders.** The relative power and influence of stakeholder groups on decision making depends on the nature of the business.

Questions

1 What is the value of information management to a business?

2 Outline the possible limitations of information management in a business context.

3 Explain scientific decision making and identify the various stages in the scientific decision-making process.

4 State the benefits of using scientific decision making.

5 What does it mean when decisions are based on hunches?

6 Why might decisions based upon hunch be used?

Managing change

7 Outline the main factors that a business might take into account when deciding whether to use scientific decision making or hunches.

8 How might a firm's ethical position influence its corporate decision making?

9 Give an example of how the availability of resources might influence a firm's corporate decision making.

10 The relative power of individual stakeholder groups and their influence on decision making depends on the nature of the business. Give four examples of how the relative power of different stakeholder groups might influence corporate decision making.

Making strategic decisions

Essay-style question

In order to answer the following question it is advisable first to undertake revision of the topic in the context of real-life businesses. Then, in the space provided, produce an outline plan of your answer. If you have time, use a separate sheet to write up the essay in full.

It took 5 years and 5,127 prototypes for James Dyson to come up with his first bagless cleaner, which started selling in Japan in 1986. Since then, Dyson has expanded the business to 37 countries and shifted his factory from England to Malaysia. The company continues to develop the technology and about a quarter of the 1,300 employees at Dyson's headquarters in England work in research and development.

Assess the extent to which the decision to move production from England to Malaysia is likely to have been based on a scientific approach to decision making rather than on the basis of Dyson's own gut instinct or hunch.

Implementing and managing change

Techniques to implement and manage change

Project champions
A **project champion** has two essential roles in relation to a project:
- to advocate and promote the benefits of pursuing the project
- to overcome funding constraints or problems with resource allocation

Desirable characteristics of a project champion include:
- involvement in the organisation's decision-making process
- a commitment to pursuing support for the project within the organisation
- good people skills and the ability to build relationships easily

Project management
Good **project management** means that things get done on time, within budget, and meet or exceed the expectations of the business.

Project groups
Project groups provide opportunities for job enlargement (as workers are often allowed to take on a variety of different tasks within the group) and synergy (because the combined results of the project group working together as a team of individuals is greater than the individual parts).

External consultants and external specialists
External consultants and specialists are often brought in when an organisation does not have the expertise itself or where its management needs to remain focused on existing business.

Factors that promote or resist change
Factors that promote or hinder change are:
- the clarity of objectives
- the appropriateness and sufficiency of resources
- the appropriateness of training
- the effectiveness of planning
- the impact on employees and how the business deals with this
- the skills and commitment of employees
- the effectiveness of teams
- the nature of the organisational structure
- external factors

Questions
Optimal Business Solutions, an IT services business, is considering significant change to its organisation in order to cut costs and improve efficiency. It has created a project group, appointed a project manager and identified a project champion. It has also contracted the services of a specialist external consultancy firm to assist the process.

Implementing and managing change

1 Identify the factors that are most likely to influence the success of the change process.

2 How might the project group contribute to the success of the project?

3 Consider the differences between the roles of the project manager and the project champion.

4 Analyse the characteristics of a good project champion and how the role of the project champion might benefit projects that aim to initiate change.

Managing change

5 Consider the likely reasons for Optimal's decision to contract the services of the specialist external consultancy.

Essay-style question

In order to answer the following question it is advisable first to undertake revision of the topic in the context of real-life businesses. Then, in the space provided, produce an outline plan of your answer. If you have time, use a separate sheet to write up the essay in full.

Evaluate the factors that might assist Optimal Business Solutions to promote the intended change and those that might impede such change.